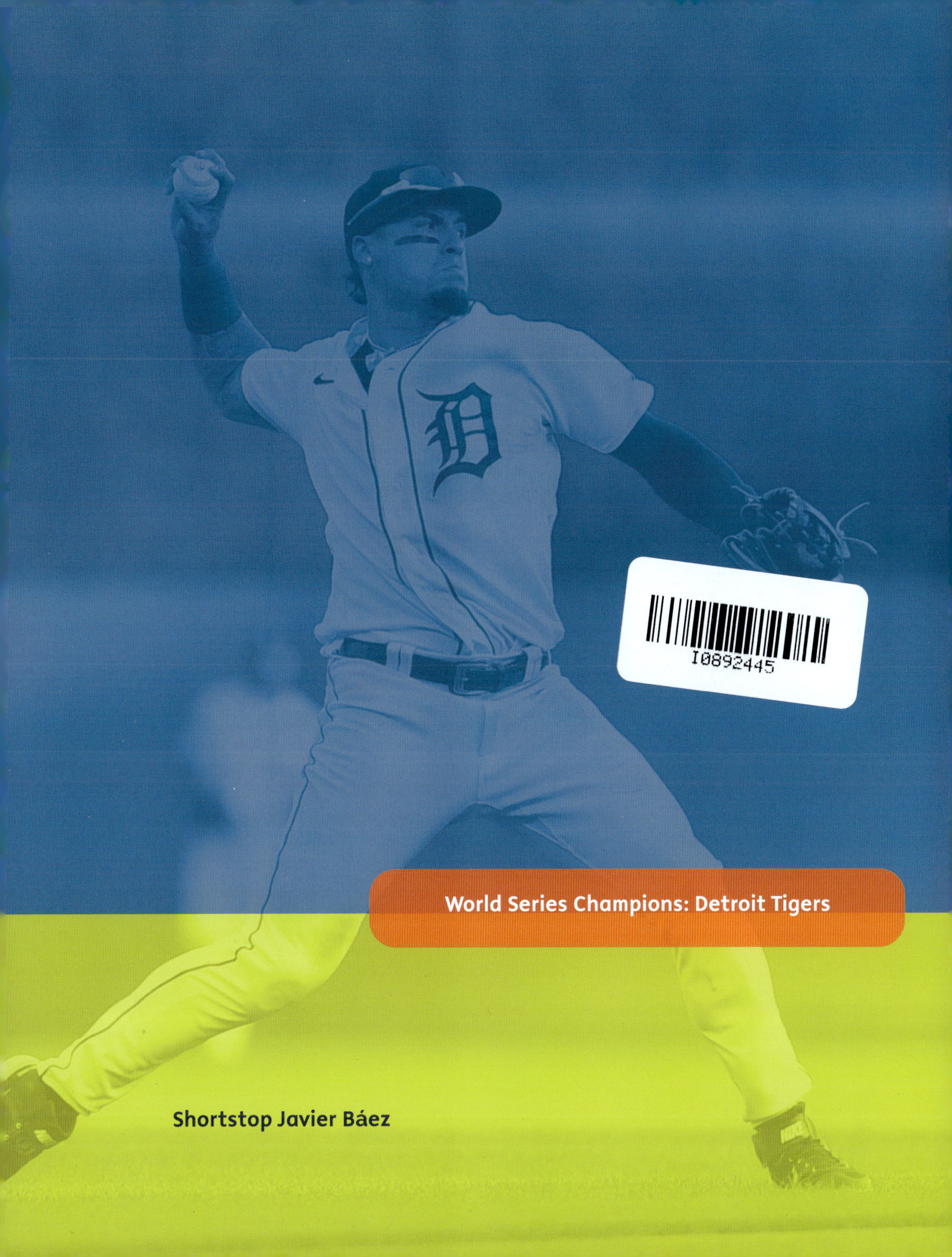

World Series Champions: Detroit Tigers

Shortstop Javier Báez

Pitcher Max Scherzer

WORLD SERIES CHAMPIONS

DETROIT TIGERS

JOE TISCHLER

CREATIVE SPORTS

CREATIVE EDUCATION / CREATIVE PAPERBACKS

Published by Creative Education and Creative Paperbacks
P.O. Box 227, Mankato, Minnesota 56002
Creative Education and Creative Paperbacks are imprints of The Creative Company
www.thecreativecompany.us

Art Direction by Tom Morgan
Book production by Ciara Beitlich
Edited by Jill Kalz

Photographs by AP Images (Associated Press, Allan Dranberg, Frank Jansky/Icon Sportswire), Getty (Getty Images Sport, Patrick McDermott, MLB Photos, National Baseball Hall of Fame, Rich Pilling, Gregory Shamus, Trancendental Graphics, ZUMA/Alamy), Shutterstock (f11photo)

Library of Congress Cataloging-in-Publication Data
Names: Tischler, Joe, author.
Title: Detroit Tigers / Joe Tischler.
Description: Mankato, MN : Creative Education and Creative Paperbacks, [2024] | Series: Creative sports. World Series champions | Includes index. | Audience: Ages 7-10 | Audience: Grades 2-3 | Summary: "Elementary-level text and engaging sports photos highlight the Detroit Tigers' MLB World Series wins and losses, plus sensational players associated with the professional baseball team such as Miguel Cabrera."-- Provided by publisher.
Identifiers: LCCN 2023008252 (print) | LCCN 2023008253 (ebook) | ISBN 9781640268227 (library binding) | ISBN 9781682773727 (paperback) | ISBN 9781640009929 (pdf)
Subjects: LCSH: Detroit Tigers (Baseball team)--History--Juvenile literature. | World Series (Baseball)--History--Juvenile literature.
Classification: LCC GV875.D6 T57 2024 (print) | LCC GV875.D6 (ebook) | DDC 796.357/640977434--dc23/eng/20230227
LC record available at https://lccn.loc.gov/2023008252
LC ebook record available at https://lccn.loc.gov/2023008253

Printed in China

1984 World Series Champions

Outfielder Al Kaline

CONTENTS

Home of the Tigers

Detroit, Michigan, is well known for its automobile industry. It's often called the "Motor City." Detroit is also known for its baseball team, the Tigers. They play at a **stadium** called Comerica Park.

The Tigers are a Major League Baseball (MLB) team. They play in the American League (AL) Central Division. Their main **rivals** are the Cleveland Guardians and Chicago White Sox. Each year, MLB teams try to get to the World Series. Only one will be crowned champion of the league.

Pitcher Tarik Skubal

Naming the Tigers

The AL was formed in 1901. One of its first teams was the Detroit Tigers. Some MLB teams have had many nicknames. Detroit's team has always been called the Tigers. One reason for the name is in reference to a Detroit military unit during the Civil War. It was nicknamed "Tigers." Tigers players wear navy blue hats with a white *D* on the front for home games. The *D* is orange when they play on the road.

Outfielder Ty Cobb

Tigers History

The Tigers were winners nearly from the start. They played in three straight World Series from 1907 to 1909. They lost them all. Ty Cobb was a star hitter during those years. He led the AL in hitting 12 times during his career. He holds the highest career batting average of all time (.366).

Detroit finally broke through with a World Series **title** in 1935! They beat the Chicago Cubs. The Tigers beat the Cubs again in the 1945 World Series. Slugger Hank Greenberg led the AL in home runs and runs batted in (RBI) four times each.

First baseman Hank Greenberg

Shortstop Alan Trammell

Pitcher Denny McLain won 31 games in 1968. He's the last MLB pitcher to win at least 30 games in a season. That year, the Tigers beat the St. Louis Cardinals to win the World Series.

In 1984, infielders Alan Trammell and Lou Whitaker helped the club win their fourth and final World Series title to date.

Other Team Stars

Slugger Miguel Cabrera came to Detroit in 2008. He led the AL in batting average four times. He even won the **Triple Crown** in 2012. He led the AL in home runs, RBI, and batting average.

First baseman Miguel Cabrera

Pitcher Justin Verlander

In the 2010s, pitchers Justin Verlander and Max Scherzer each won a Cy Young Award. The award is given to the league's best pitcher. These stars helped the Tigers reach two World Series in the 2000s.

New pitchers Casey Mize and Tarik Skubal hope to bring more World Series banners to Comerica Park soon. Fans hope so, too!

About the Tigers

Started playing: 1901

League/division: American League, Central Division

Team colors: navy, blue, and orange

Home stadium: Comerica Park

WORLD SERIES CHAMPIONSHIPS:

1935, 4 games to 2 over Chicago Cubs

1945, 4 games to 3 over Chicago Cubs

1968, 4 games to 3 over St. Louis Cardinals

1984, 4 games to 1 over San Diego Padres

Detroit Tigers website: www.mlb.com/tigers

Glossary

rival—a team that plays extra hard against another team

stadium—a building with tiers of seats for spectators

title—another word for championship

Triple Crown—the honor of leading the league in three different categories in the same season

Outfielder Harry Heilmann

Index